WILLIAM SHAKESPEARE

The
PROBLEM PLAYS

Troilus and Cressida · All's Well That Ends Well
Measure for Measure · Timon of Athens

by
PETER URE

Published for the British Council and
The National Book league by
LONGMANS GREEN & CO.

LONGMANS, GREEN & CO. LTD.
48 Grosvenor Street, London W.1
Thibault House, Thibault Square, Cape Town
605–611 Lonsdale Street, Melbourne C.1.

LONGMANS, GREEN & CO. INC.
119 West 40th Street, New York 18

LONGMANS, GREEN & CO.
20 Cranfield Road, Toronto 16

ORIENT LONGMANS LTD.
Calcutta Bombay Madras
Delhi Hyderabad Dacca

Printed in Great Britain by
F. Mildner & Sons, London, E.C.1

CONTENTS

I THE PROBLEM PLAYS   *page* 7

II ALL'S WELL THAT ENDS WELL   8

III MEASURE FOR MEASURE   18

IV TROILUS AND CRESSIDA   32

V TIMON OF ATHENS   44

VI CONCLUSION   52

     A Select Bibliography   54

ILLUSTRATIONS

(between pages 30 and 31)

I TIMON OF ATHENS: the frontispiece to Rowe's
edition, 1709.   *Angus McBean*

II ALL'S WELL THAT ENDS WELL: a scene from
Tyrone Guthrie's production at the Shakespeare Memorial
Theatre, Stratford-upon-Avon, 1959, decor by Tanya Moi-
seiwitsch.

III MEASURE FOR MEASURE: from a design for the
play by John Piper, reproduced by his kind permission.
     Houston Rogers

IV TROILUS AND CRESSIDA: a scene from Tyrone
Guthrie's production at the Old Vic, 1956, with designs by
Frederick Crooke.

¶ Acknowledgement is due to the guidance given in *Shakespeare and
the Artist* by Professor W. Moelwyn Merchant (O.U.P., 1959), and
to courtesies extended by the author.

¶ WILLIAM SHAKESPEARE was born at Stratford-on-Avon and was christened in the Parish Church on 26 April 1564. There, too, he died, on 23 April 1616, and was buried in the chancel, where a monument was erected before 1623.

SHAKESPEARE

I

THE PROBLEM PLAYS

THE term 'problem plays' was first applied to *All's Well, Measure for Measure*, and *Troilus and Cressida* by F. S. Boas (who associated *Hamlet* with them) in 1896. It is not a term which bears too rigorous an examination. Boas had in mind the analogy with such plays as Ibsen's, dealing with social injustices and their effects on the lives of individuals. The analogy is not a perfect one for the plays discussed here. But Boas's phrase has proved hard to dispense with, and is now an accepted label for a group of plays which have some features in common: the probing of character under the test of situations which raise conflicting ethical interpretations; the replacement of the strain of occasional melancholy which is found even in Shakespeare's most festive comedies by an urgently satirical and disfiguring temper; a willingness even in comedy to draw near to pain and death; a curious interweaving of romantic and even fantastic tales with realistic characterization, which itself sometimes moves towards allegory and symbol; an art whose occasional apparent contempt and carelessness about what W. B. Yeats called the 'wheels and pulleys' of drama, the machinery for achieving consistency and smooth running, mediate the reach and pressure of a mind profoundly aware that energy and meaning in the theatre may spring from the attempt to embody in its forms the very resistance which life offers to being translated into the expressive modes of art. In these plays, drama seems to grow up into recognizing the stuff it is made from, just as the modern sculptor consciously preserves the roughness and accidental flaws of metal or stone in order to signalize the obstinate survival of the material in the artefact. What,

apart from these general features, are the individual
'problems' of the problem plays will, it is hoped, emerge
in the accounts that follow. But it ought to be added here
that their language is often extremely hard to construe. It
is tough and subtle, compounded of unexpected words,
daring and resonant images, and strangely subterranean
and occluded rhythms. For all readers this is the first and
most vital 'problem'.

The dates of all four plays, except *Measure for Measure*
(which was probably written not long before its first
recorded performance at court on December 26, 1604) are
uncertain. The following is a conjectural sequence: *Hamlet*
(*c*.1601); *The Merry Wives of Windsor* (*c*. 1602); *TROILUS
AND CRESSIDA* (*c*. 1602); *ALL'S WELL THAT ENDS
WELL* (*c*. 1603); *Othello* (1604); *TIMON OF ATHENS*
(1605 or 1608-9); *King Lear* (1605-6); *Macbeth* (1606);
Antony and Cleopatra (1608).

II

ALL'S WELL THAT ENDS WELL

Those who saw Tyrone Guthrie's production of *All's Well*
at Stratford-on-Avon in 1959 will remember it as a cool
and gracious, blue and silver affair, stately and Ruritanian
and somewhat withdrawn in its general effect. These
elements are of course present in the play; but there are
others which belie them. The problem of *All's Well* is to
some extent the problem of reconciling much gracious
calm and ageing wisdom in the persons of Bertram's mother
and Helena's guardian (the Countess of Rousillon), the
old lord Lafew, and the King of France himself, with much
unhewn acerbity and youthful drive in the persons of Helena
and Bertram. They are hero and heroine of a play which
does not hold these two roles in any very clearly perceived
balance. It is Helena's love for Bertram which motivates

the entire action; and within Helena there are found in puzzling proportions both maidenly modesty and a determination to get what she wants. Indeed, any one element seems to have its opposite somewhere else in the play. The topsy-turviness which at once strikes us—that it is the woman who seeks the man—is productive of dilemmas for the major characters that bite destructively into their dignity however much a performance on the stage may stress the courtliness of their milieu. Shakespeare was writing at a time when there was a fashion for play-titles in the form of proverbs, but in another age, that of Pinero or Galsworthy, he might well have called this strange comedy not *All's Well that Ends Well* but *Embarrassments*.

Shakespeare took his story from Boccaccio's *Decameron* (the ninth *novella* of the third day) as he found it either in the French version of Antoine le Maçon or the English version of William Painter (*The Palace of Pleasure*, probably the third edition of 1575). Possibly he consulted both, but the atmosphere of the play, as G. K. Hunter has observed, is decidedly French (even if it is that part of France which borders on Ruritania). Shakespeare has cropped the original narrative in the interest of theatrical speed and has in some places deepened the sense of embarrassing reality; and he has added new characters, the Countess and her clown and her attendant lord Lafew. Parolles and his under-plot is Shakespeare's invention, too, although their part of the story is not more than a variation on the traditional story of the *miles gloriosus*, popular in comedy since Roman times. Essentially the tale remains that of the physician's orphaned daughter Helena (Boccaccio's Giletta) who falls in love with her guardian's son Count Bertram (Boccaccio's Beltramo). When Bertram's father dies, the young Count is summoned to the court at Paris, and Helena, hearing that the king is afflicted with an abscess which none of his doctors can cure, follows Bertram to court armed with her father's sovereign elixir. The king, at first sceptical, is at length persuaded to try her medicine; if it fails, Helena is to die unpleasantly; if it succeeds, the king will give her the husband whom she chooses. The king is restored to health and freshness as by a 'heavenly effect', with the miraculous felicity of folk-tale; but when the time comes for husband-choosing, Bertram halts the smooth and lovely progress of the fable with vivid embarrassment:

> *King*.   Know'st thou not, Bertram,
> What has she done for me?
> *Ber*.   Yes, my good lord;
> But never hope to know why I should marry her.
> *King*. Thou know'st she has rais'd me from my sickly bed.
> *Ber*. But follows it, my lord, to bring me down
> Must answer for your raising? I know her well:
> She had her breeding at my father's charge.
> A poor physician's daughter my wife! Disdain
> Rather corrupt me ever! (II.iii. 106–13).[1]

Immune to the king's philosophically stated promise that he will make Bertram's wife socially worthy of Bertram's nobility (she has earned the title of honour by her own acts and worth), he finally has to yield sullenly to the king's open anger. Everyone, except his vulgar and loud-mouthed follower Parolles, is disgusted with his failure to live up to the situation. Even Helena, otherwise silent during the storm, tries to withdraw:

> That you are well restor'd, my lord, I'm glad.
> Let the rest go.

Immediately after the wedding-ceremony the new-married Count, with Parolles's encouragement, deserts his wife for the Italian wars. He hates her, nothing less (II.iii.280), and in one cold farewell interview gives her a letter imposing impossible conditions for their union:

> When thou canst get the ring upon my finger, which never shall come off, and show me a child begotten of thy body that I am father to, then call me husband; but to such a "then" I write a "never".

[1]All quotations from Shakespeare are from *The Complete Works*, ed. Peter Alexander (London, 1951).

It is at this point, the lowest of her fortunes, that Helena makes her great speech of love, resolution, and independence, a speech in which, as Dr. Tillyard has said, Shakespeare's imagination was, so far as this play goes, uniquely kindled:

> O you leaden messengers,
> That ride upon the violent speed of fire,
> Fly with false aim; move the still-piecing air,
> That sings with piercing; do not touch my lord.
> Whoever shoots at him, I set him there;
> Whoever charges on his forward breast,
> I am the caitiff that do hold him to't;
> And though I kill him not, I am the cause
> His death was so effected. Better 'twere
> I met the ravin lion when he roar'd
> With sharp constraint of hunger; better 'twere
> That all the miseries which nature owes
> Were mine at once. No; come thou home, Rousillon,
> Whence honour but of danger wins a scar,
> As oft it loses all. I will be gone.
> My being here it is that holds thee hence.
> Shall I stay here to do't? No, no, although
> The air of paradise did fan the house,
> And angels offic'd all.   (III. ii. 107–25)

Such a speech was badly needed at this juncture. It is a fine example of that most important of all units in Shakespearian composition, the long, exacting speech highly charged with metaphor, highly revelatory of the speaker's passionate soul, truly 'miming her psyche', and yet at the same time looking forward, filled with preparation for future action. It is the pivot of the play; or, rather, the lever with which Helena starts to lift her second immense burden, the true conquest of Bertram, which is the business of the remaining two and a half Acts. It serves, too, to make the point that it is difficult to tell the story of the first half of the play without making it seem that it is Bertram's re-actions and state of mind which count for reader and playgoer. But it is really Helena to whom our attention is

directed. We see the gracious setting of her adopted home,
to which she returns as it were to a haven of gentle sympathies and comforting indignation when all seems lost at
court; and earlier, in the first Act, before the visit to Paris,
we are present when the Countess, with all the sympathy
of wise feminine affection for youth caught in a sexual
trap, uncovers Helena's secret passion for her son (I. iii. 119
ff., a scene which has no counterpart in the source). By the
most delicate touches and in writing characteristic of
Shakespeare's mature style, in which richness of figure is
wonderfully combined with colloquial vigour and continuous dependence on rhythms that convey a living
presence, the Countess invades Helena's personality:

> I say I am your mother,
> And put you in the catalogue of those
> That were enwombed mine. 'Tis often seen
> Adoption strives with nature, and choice breeds
> A native slip to us from foreign seeds.
> You ne'er oppressed me with a mother's groan,
> Yet I express to you a mother's care.
> God's mercy, maiden! does it curd thy blood
> To say I am thy mother? What's the matter
> That this distempered messenger of wet,
> The many-colour'd Iris, rounds thine eye?   (I. iii. 133–43)

For Helena, it is a torture of embarrassment, of blushes and
tears, and of final release in avowal. This scene, occurring
early in the play, sets her firmly and for ever in the centre
of our imaginative concern. Bertram the hero (and his
denomination as such now takes on an ironic sound) is
never given anything so interesting to do or to be. In
rejecting the Helena about whom we know so much, he
both affronts us and serves us in a way that makes it difficult
to take him as other than either a case of youthful conceit
about whom we can always be detached, or as a necessary
component of Helena's fable of impossible tasks triumphantly
accomplished in the manner of Psyche, who also drew the
sting of Love's malignancy. I do not see how any historical

criticism, in terms of Bertram's rights as a nobleman or of once potent ideas about what such a man might have expected his marriage to do for him in the world, can affect the knowledge and concern that are given to Helena as a result of the painful and touching interview with her 'mother'.

Even in the scene where Bertram's choice means a great deal, he is strangely subordinate. As Helena, 'choosing' her husband, walks along the line of gentlemen in a dance of courtship, and they respond with affection and desire, Bertram is there plainly just to be different. Later in the scene, our interest is in the king's strong lines about Honour and in the force and consistency of his motives. His speech, demonstrating that Honour derives from honourable acts and not from the 'lying trophy' of an aristocratic name, solidly prepares for his declaration that his own honour is at stake if the promise which he made to Helena cannot be redeemed because of Bertram's obstinacy. Bertram cringes; and is not given the chance to reply that an Honour which depends upon the constraint of the subject is a luxury peculiar to kings.

We can afford up to this point to take Bertram as he comes, as part of Helena's story. We see his inward motives out of the corner of our eyes, and our full attention is kept away from him in the first half of the play. That he has not yet grown up is hinted; the king on their first meeting assumes that he is not yet as good a man as his dead father, but may become so. The case is otherwise with Helena. Act I. tells us all about her inward self, her terribly awkward situation, her sense of the deep gulf between herself and a Bertram silently worshipped, her clear understanding of the kind of story she is in: one in which impossibilities *must* be murdered. It is this understanding that gives her an extra dimension possessed by none of the other characters, and lends precision to her foreknowledge of her peculiar destiny. When the Countess asks how she, 'a poor unlearned virgin', can hope to cure the king when the congregated

college of physicians has withdrawn from the case, she says
of her father's medicine: 'There's something in't/More than
my father's skill.' That something is the sanctification of
heaven upon her legacy. And so, when Helena sets herself
to persuade the king of the virtue of the cure, Shakespeare
modifies the predominant style of the play to give her the
speech of a prophet and miracle-worker:

> It is not so with Him that all things knows
> As 'tis with us that square our guess by shows.

It is not difficult to reconcile this remote, thaumaturgic
heroine with the passionate girl of the first Act. For her
conscious assumption of the miracle-worker's role springs
from her realization that she has a place in a miracle-story.
For this space of time she deliberately transforms herself
into her father's legatee, the bearer of his mysterious gift.
The king acknowledges that something unearthly transmits
its voice through the mask which Helena has assumed:

> Methinks in thee some blessed spirit doth speak
> His powerful sound within an organ weak;
> And what impossibility would slay
> In common sense, sense saves another way.   (II. ii. 174–7)

We see, therefore, in the first half of the play the making
of a heroine of a peculiarly Shakespearian kind. Like
Perdita, Miranda, Hermione, or Imogen, she can participate
in the working out of what Thomas Mann's Joseph called
a wonderful God-story without losing her human linea-
ments, her charm, her sensuousness, her anxiety, her sharp
sense of what it is to live as a human being by antilogies
which defy common calculation but can only be resolved
by some marvellous event:

> O, then, give pity
> To her whose state is such that cannot choose
> But lend and give where she is sure to lose;
> That seeks not to find that her search implies,
> But, riddle-like, lives sweetly where she dies! (I. iii. 204–8)

It is the great puzzle of *All's Well* that, although the antilogies *are* resolved and the right total given at the foot of the page—Helena gets Bertram at the very end of the fifth Act—we do not feel that the sum has been done in the most elegant and convincing way. It is putting it too crudely to say that the wonder-working heroine of the first Acts is transformed into a business-woman in the later ones. The Helena of the later part is withdrawn a good deal from our knowledge altogether. When she does appear (most importantly in III.vii and IV.iv) she combines a little moral reflection with a great deal of merely arranging matters for the fulfilment of the conditions imposed by Bertram in his outrageous letter. Her instruments (and they are in themselves little more) are the Florentine widow and her daughter Diana, whom Bertram is trying to seduce. Without his knowledge, Helena substitutes herself for Diana in Bertram's bed; in the complex *dénouement* this achievement and her identity are proved in a series of rational revelations by token and witness. But the Helena who is the key to the narrative and, technically speaking, still the absolutely un-challenged mover of the plot, has become even more neutral and subordinate than Bertram was in the first Acts, although the burden of 'impossibilities' that she is lifting is now much greater.

One explanation for the change in direction may be that Shakespeare had a long story yet to tell, and perhaps the more difficult of his two stories to recast in theatrical form. But much space and time that might have been devoted to a less business-like and unactualized representation of the second story are stolen by the attention now given to Parolles. It has also been argued that in the later part of the play we see something of development in Bertram, that the kind of interest in the human personage and its relation to the story in which it finds itself which grows up round Helena in the first Acts transfers itself to Bertram in the later ones. The sense that Bertram is young and raw and therefore capable of growing, the subordination of Helena, and the new military and masculine setting, all suggest that Shakespeare may be turning the play in this direction. In the first part, as we have seen, we do not feel the need to blame Bertram very much for his shabby behaviour. (Everyone agrees that it is shabby, and his motive—Helena's humble birth—is declared invalid by the king's potent authority as philosopher and monarch.) It is Helena who focuses our interest, and we suspend judgement on Bertram because of our (perhaps never very openly acknowledged) feeling that he must behave thus for the story to be continued. But we have now entered his world, the world of Florence and the wars, one in which Helena is essentially a stranger. Bertram is able to be freer of the constrictions of the story, and it would accord with Shakespeare's art that some process which might be entitled 'the education of Bertram' should now be set afoot—something which would rescue him from the brutalities forced upon him by the tale and perhaps help to show us why Helena finds him so attractive. Certainly Bertram has an adventure, not allowed for in the source. Characteristically, it is at someone else's expense: that of his companion, Parolles.

It is this adventure which, it has been argued, Shakespeare uses to show us a Bertram 'thoroughly shaken' by consciousness of his folly and fear of what is to come.[1] It is true that Bertram's limited insight cannot penetrate to Parolles's true nature long after others are suspecting him; it is true that Parolles tends to encourage Bertram's selfishness and desertion (II. iii. 260 ff), with his 'A young man married is a man that's marr'd' and 'The King has done you wrong'. But there is nothing that links Parolles with Bertram in such a way as to suggest that he is Bertram's 'evil genius', or that his unmasking as a cowardly braggart in one of the most brilliantly theatrical scenes (IV.iii) par-

[1] E. M. W. Tillyard, *Shakespeare's Problem Plays* (1950), p. 116. A more elaborate account on these lines is given in Bertrand Evans's *Shakespeare's Comedies* (1960); but Evans seems to me to be talking about a play Shakespeare might have written rather than the one he actually did write.

takes of an educative process that helps Bertram to grow up, to realize what he himself is, and that his 'Honour' has feet of clay. Dr Tillyard is able to read 'inner qualms' and 'sullen anger' into the few and rather colourless words given to Bertram during this long scene; but his longest speech (IV. iii. 81–7) seems to express only brisk self-satisfaction combined with anticipation of sexual enjoyment (his plans for the seduction of Diana are now, he thinks, well forward). The scene itself is wonderfully managed, but it is wholly Parolles's. G. K. Hunter has written of the Jonsonian excess of the character and of the 'Jonsonian deflation in the cruel horseplay'. Parolles is depicted by methods that hardly suit with the rest of the play and certainly do not minister to Bertram's moral needs.

Of such needs he shows no consciousness; the Bertram who proceeds to his own unmasking in Act V appears to have learnt nothing from Parolles's fate. The opportunity to use two rather similar scenic processes, in juxtaposition to one another, in order to deepen either's meaning is one which it is surprising to find Shakespeare letting slip. For in the final scene of exposure Bertram twists and turns until the last possible moment, until he is stunned by the appearance of Helena, whom everyone had supposed to be dead. Just as the passion of Helena runs like a vein of metal through the first Act, so does the callousness of Bertram through the last. We are obliged to accept, because of the traditional nature of the story, the belief that all's well that ends well. But it only needs a slight shift of perspective, and one which keeps many elements in the play still perfectly focused, for us to start wondering whether this acceptance is possible only because of the de-characterization of Helena that has occurred in the second half. Yet if the Helena of the first Act has now been supplanted by the Clever Wench of folk-tale,[1] no such transformation has taken place in

---

[1] See especially W. W. Lawrence's account in *Shakespeare's Problem Comedies* (1931).

Bertram. Altogether a darker figure than Boccaccio's hero[1] he has now acquired such a reality of stubbornly consistent shabbiness and lack of bounty that what is worrying is not Helena's fate at his hands (for *that* Helena can only be recalled with an unnatural effort) but the thought that two characters from two quite disparate kinds of fiction are pretending that they belong to the same world. As the bells of comedy ring out, this is perhaps not of enormous importance, but the pretence does not suffice to bring the two worlds together, and makes the ending of the play somewhat less than satisfying.

III

MEASURE FOR MEASURE

When we turn from *All's Well* to *Measure for Measure* it soon becomes clear that the two comedies resemble one another but that their differences are just as interesting as their likenesses. One indication of a contrast in mood and execution is supplied by the comic characters. The Clown and Parolles in *All's Well* do not seem much to enjoy their lives or to minister to the play's chief events. The Clown is not a success, and while it is true that Parolles in the scene of his unmasking shows a vigorous facility for ruining himself which outgoes even the expectations of his captors, his fear implicates us all in his shame: we witness as it were the judicial murder of a dramatic character,[2] and at no point is his ebullience other than nervous: 'he does not really believe in himself.'[3] But the comic personages in *Measure*

---

[1] On this point see G. K. Hunter's New Arden edition, pp. xxvi–vii.

[2] We witness, too—and it is a great, though not finally a permanent, relief—his resurrection in his soliloquy at the end of the scene (IV.iii), which contains the famous and (perhaps irrelevantly) moving line: 'Simply the thing I am shall make me live.'

[3] See G. K. Hunter, New Arden edition, p. xlvii.

for Measure—Lucio, Mistress Overdone, Pompey—do believe in themselves. Although they live under the shadow of magistrates and policemen and other professional punishers and guardians of our moral rectitude they still manage to relish their lives: 'it is not a question of whether we like Pompey, but of whether Pompey likes himself.'[1] Amidst much in the play that is sombre or exalted, Pompey and his fellows remind us that *Measure for Measure* is, after all, a comedy, and Shakespeare plants richly in the centre of his drama their abundant delight in the comforts of life; it is the man of undeveloped heart who finds them boring or disgusting and would like to have them whipped (II. i. 131). This vital delight in his own existence, carrying with it a certain imperturbability, would seem indeed to be the comic character's first ground of appeal to his audience, as Charlie Chaplin or M. Hulot or Tony Hancock continually demonstrate.

Yet, though there are contrasts of this kind, there are also many likenesses, and it is these that will strike home first. In both plays an eloquent young girl is an absolutely central figure and is subjected to a series of tests; in both there is a judge to whom the final appeal is made in the course of complex fifth-act *dénouements*; in both there is the 'bed-trick', the substitution of one woman for another without the man's awareness of the change; and in both the major characters are threatened by disaster and loss after the manner of tragi-comedy. But *Measure for Measure* is a play with a much sharper appeal, a more unified and more exciting story, and a far greater reach of mind than *All's Well*. This has had its repercussions in criticism. Dr Leavis has called the play a 'controlled experiment', and it does seem to conduct an experiment not only on the characters within it but on all its spectators. It leaves us with a sense that we, too, are being subjected to a peculiarly rigorous test of our capacity for making a true judgement. Conse-

[1] Mary Lascelles, *Shakespeare's Measure for Measure* (1953), p. 159.

quently it has inspired a very large body of criticism (probably larger than for any other of Shakespeare's comedies), and this criticism is very far from speaking with a single voice. Any account of *Measure for Measure* may be wrecked on one reef or another. It is some hint at the deeps and difficulties of this comedy that its proverb-like title carries a direct allusion to the Sermon on the Mount:

> Give and it shall be given unto you: a good measure, pressed down, shaken together, and running over shall men give into your bosom: for with what measure you mete, with the same shall men mete to you again.

Yet it has been a major cause of complaint that such even-handed justice is singularly baffled in the play's resolution, which affords pardon to its chief evildoer.

Shakespeare's principal source was George Whetstone's clumsily elaborate old play in two parts *Promos and Cassandra* (1578). In a Hungarian city whose magistrate the Lord Promos is conducting a reign of legal terror and corruption, Cassandra's brother Andrugio is condemned to death for 'loving too kindly'. Cassandra's appeal to the judge for mercy is first rejected, then accepted on condition that she becomes his mistress. To save her brother Cassandra finally agrees, but Promos goes back on the bargain and orders the gaoler to execute Andrugio and send his head to his sister. The gaoler disobeys, substituting the mangled head of another felon; but Cassandra, believing it to be her brother's, appeals to the King for justice against Promos, who is finally condemned first to marry the woman he has wronged and then to die. Cassandra now seeks mercy for her husband, but it is granted only when Andrugio steps forward alive, when a general pardon ensues. Shakespeare borrowed the main narrative idea from Whetstone's play, which also corresponds with Shakespeare's in having a comic underplot of low life in the city. But he transformed by many radical changes a story which has rightly been called shallow and barbarous. His Isabella (= Cassandra) is a novice in a convent who pleads with but cannot yield to Angelo (= Promos); his Duke of Vienna (Whetstone's King), disguised as a friar, knows what is going on from the beginning of the action. He is responsible both for saving the life of the brother (Claudio) and for deceiving Angelo into thinking that Isabella has consented to his desires by arranging for the substitution in his bed of Angelo's betrothed Mariana (a new character). This last device was doubtless suggested by the similar trick in *All's Well*, while the notion of a disguised ruler controlling the action from within had been used in three of Marston's plays and in one of Middleton's, and in many other places, including of course the *Arabian Nights*. The story used by Whetstone appears in various other forms during the sixteenth century, including Giraldi's *Hecatommithi*, a collection of *novelle* which also contains the story of *Othello* (1565), and the commentators believe that Shakespeare knew several of them. From this material, and using a mixture of realistic and symbolic techniques matched, if at all, only by *King Lear* and *The Tempest*, he devised a comedy which seems, in Miss Lascelles's words, to 'liberate thoughts impatient of confinement', thoughts about mercy and justice and sexual morality, and yet all the time confines them not only within a pattern of events but within a series of sharply individualized characters, who have always strongly aroused the impulse to praise or to blame.

The play does not really catch fire until the second scene of the second act. Here Angelo and Isabella meet for the first time in a naked conflict of principle, which springs so strangely from Shakespeare's 'Vienna', with its bawds and easy livers, and Elbow, its inefficient Elizabethan policeman. His design up to this point is fairly clear and indisputable. The Duke has withdrawn from Vienna, leaving the state in charge of his deputy Angelo. He has two related motives for this act of seeming abdication: to use Angelo to the full while testing him:

> Heaven doth with us as we with torches do,
> Not light them for themselves; for if our virtues
> Did not go forth of us, 'twere all alike
> As if we had them not. Spirits are not finely touch'd
> But to fine issues; nor Nature never lends
> The smallest scruple of her excellence
> But, like a thrifty goddess, she determines
> Herself the glory of a creditor,
> Both thanks and use.   (I. i. 32–41)

The use to which Angelo is to be put is to tighten up the laws, which, as the Duke later explains (I.iii), have been slackly administered; but he has not simply abandoned his own responsibility, and remains in disguise in the midst of all in order to discover how his plan works out. Like other people in the play, the Duke has an opinion about Angelo, which he does not express to his face, for that would have been to spoil the conditions of the test. Angelo is not stated to be a great expert on the government and institutions of the city (although Escalus, Angelo's own deputy, is). The impression he makes is from the start one of coldness and inhumanity; the Duke says:

> Lord Angelo is precise;
> Stands at a guard with envy; scarce confesses
> That his blood flows, or that his appetite
> Is more to bread than stone. Hence shall we see,
> If power change purpose, what our seemers be.

A more biased critic, Lucio, seconds this ('a man whose blood/Is very snow-broth'); but it is indicative of Shakespeare's essentially dramatic method that Angelo is already being seen in the context of his deeds, which, like a stone plunged into a pool, have already caused widening ripples of criticism and dismay all over Vienna. The revival of the laws against sexual immorality has upset the trade in vice. Shakespeare treats even these traders with an imaginative regard which releases a common pattern of feeling: that it is 'us' (ordinary people who get on as best they may) versus 'them' (the unreasonable state, the inexplicable decisions of governors, embodied, in this case, in Angelo). 'Truly, sir, I am a poor fellow that would live', says Pompey, and the claim remains an unanswerable one, even in a play that is so much occupied with the quality rather than the mere continuance of the individual life. More importantly, we are concerned with Claudio's fate, who is to die for getting his betrothed, Juliet, with child. His is a special case. Angelo is legally justified in exacting the penalty; but everyone, including the expert Escalus, agrees that it is cruel and risky to do so. Claudio and Juliet were wrong and feel guilt and shame because, while their contraction of a clandestine marriage (consisting of a simple declaration that they are husband and wife) was legally admissible in Elizabethan times, the Church disapproved of such marriages and especially regarded their consummation before they had been publicly solemnized as a sin.[1] But to take a man's life for it is tyrannical. With that curious personalization of the issue which is central to drama, although it would seem odd in real life, Escalus wonders if Angelo is really so remote from such temptations himself as to be entitled to go as far he proposes to go in condemning Claudio. The point is duly recognized even in our own administrative and legal systems. The personal lives of judges must be austere, and even lawmakers and parliament-men are disqualified from office if they are caught in a personal scandal. But we would think it strange to question a perfectly legal decision by asking the judge (as Angelo is repeatedly asked) whether he feels so sure that *he* could never commit a crime. This is indeed the first thing that the characters in the play think of in relation to Angelo. That Shakespeare is both writing a comedy and at the same time deeply questioning the institutions that are supposed to embody our concepts of morality is vividly demonstrated in all that follows. For the question 'Are you

[1] See E. Schanzer, 'The Marriage-Contracts in *Measure for Measure*', *Shakespeare Survey*, XIII, (1960), 81–9.

so good that you can afford to condemn another?' ('Judge
not that ye be not judged') is one which, pressed home,
would make all our legal arrangements impossible. We
cannot imagine anyone answering 'Yes' (Angelo certainly
does not): yet the answer 'No' does not carry with it, in
practice, a refusal to condemn, to build prisons and scaffolds.
The whole question of what place Mercy has in Law is
raised but not determined in this part of the play, because,
as it turns out, Angelo is involved in a personal scandal
which, even on the lowest view, disqualifies him for
judicial office. He should have been merciful not because
all men, even the uprightest judges, should always be merciful (and what then would happen to Law?), but because he
himself will need mercy, and for a specific fault, which
resembles the one he is punishing now. Thus, it may be
said, Angelo's wickedness saves the comedy—saves Claudio
since the Duke is freed by Angelo's crime to take out-of-
court action against the wicked judge—and by introducing
the question of Angelo's own crime supersedes the problem
of Claudio's.

It is into the heady air of such issues that Isabella and
Angelo move in their first clash (II.ii). There is good
reason to believe, with Dr. Schanzer, that Shakespeare
intended us to suppose that Isabella thinks that Claudio's
crime is plain fornication, the vice she most abhors (II.ii. 29)
as a novice vowed to chastity. Her appeal to Angelo,
although it also includes the plea that the vice is a common
one, is primarily of a religious nature. All men need mercy,
even Angelo himself:

> Why, all the souls that were were forfeit once;
> And he that might the vantage best have took
> Found out the remedy. How would you be
> If He, which is the top of judgement, should
> But judge you as you are? O, think on that;
> And mercy then will breathe within your lips,
> Like man new made.   (II.ii. 73–9)

She urges him:

> Go to your bosom,
> Knock there, and ask your heart what it doth know
> That's like my brother's fault. If it confess
> A natural guiltiness such as is his,
> Let it not sound a thought upon your tongue
> Against my brother's life.   (II. ii. 136–41)

Angelo is in a way spared from wholly meeting this point (and so are all the play's spectators) because his senses have already been aroused by Isabella's presence. With shocked self-horror, he recognizes an element of perversion in the attraction which he finds in virtue and modesty in distress:

> Can it be
> That modesty may more betray our sense
> Than woman's lightness? Having waste ground enough,
> Shall we desire to raze the sanctuary,
> And pitch our evils there? O fie, fie, fie!
> What dost thou, or what art thou, Angelo?
> Dost thou desire her foully for those things
> That make her good?   (II. ii. 168–75)

There is no reason to suppose that Shakespeare wants us to think of Angelo as a natural hypocrite who has so far successfully taken everyone in, and W. W. Lawrence is certainly mistaken in describing him as 'conceived as a villain by nature, not as a good man gone wrong through sudden temptation'. But his virtue has been of a strained and cold variety, and its precarious balance is now upset.[1] He becomes a near-tragic figure, and eventually perhaps, when he orders the hasty execution of Claudio and meditates on his own situation (IV. iv. 16–32), sinks into real panic, although he recovers from this later on and puts on a fairly brazen front.

In the great scenes that follow the two confrontations of Isabella with Angelo (which occupy II.ii and iv), attention is given especially to Isabella. Around her there springs up a whole set of fresh issues from which she too is saved, like her brother Claudio, in the nick of comic time. For unless

[1] See the citations given by K. Muir, *Shakespeare's Sources I* (1957), p. 107.

that time had moved on, unless the Duke had been enabled
to step in and cut the knot, she could not have been rescued
from being a tragic figure, trapped betweens her brother's
death and the vice she most abhors. When Angelo makes his
.monstrous offer to spare her brother on condition that she
becomes his mistress, her duty is plain to her and she also
believes that Claudio will find it easier to die if he knows
that he can save her honour by doing so:

> I'll to my brother.
> Though he hath fall'n by prompture of the blood,
> Yet hath he in him such a mind of honour
> That, had he twenty heads to tender down
> On twenty bloody blocks, he'd yield them up
> Before his sister should her body stoop
> To such abhorr'd pollution.
> Then, Isabel, live chaste, and, brother, die:
> More than our brother is our chastity.
> I'll tell him yet of Angelo's request,
> And fit his mind to death, for his soul's rest.   (II. iv. 177–87)

This resolution generates a strange paradox. It is so typical
of the antithetical working of this play as to suggest that
Shakespeare is playing a game with us. He sharpens the
issues by inviting us to ask 'And what if . . .', and then rules
our question out of order with the guillotine of comedy
and by the working of a Providence (through the Duke)
which suspends the problem just when it is raised by
continuing to move towards the happy ending of comic
story. For Isabella's reading of Claudio's—or perhaps any
man's—mind in his situation is quite off the mark. When
Isabella visits him in prison, Claudio, who sees no chance
of life, has resigned himself to death as the result of the
famous *consolatio* offered him by the Duke, a speech which,
coming from a supposed Friar, raises many problems about
the pagan detachment of its tone, but which may be quoted
here as fairly to be considered the very roof and crown of
the tradition of the classical consolation—a tradition which
was much cultivated by Shakespeare and the other Eliza-

bethan dramatists, who were assiduous readers of Cicero
and Seneca:

> Be absolute for death; either death or life
> Shall thereby be the sweeter. Reason thus with life.
> If I do lose thee, I do lose a thing
> That none but fools would keep. A breath thou art,
> Servile to all the skyey influences,
> That dost this habitation where thou keep'st
> Hourly afflict. Merely, thou art Death's fool;
> For him thou labour'st by thy flight to shun
> And yet run'st toward him still. Thou art not noble;
> For all th'accommodations that thou bear'st
> Are nurs'd by baseness, Thou'rt by no means valiant;
> For thou dost fear the soft and tender fork
> Of a poor worm. Thy best of rest is sleep,
> And that thou oft provok'st; yet grossly fear'st
> Thy death, which is no more. Thou art not thyself;
> For thou exists on many a thousand grains
> That issue out of dust. Happy thou art not;
> For what thou hast not, still thou striv'st to get,
> And what thou hast, forget'st. Thou art not certain;
> For thy complexion shifts to strange effects,
> After the moon. If thou art rich, thou'rt poor;
> For, like an ass whose back with ingots bows,
> Thou bear'st thy heavy riches but a journey,
> And Death unloads thee. Friend hast thou none;
> For thine own bowels which do call thee sire,
> The mere effusion of thy proper loins,
> Do curse the gout, serpigo, and the rheum,
> For ending thee no sooner. Thou hast nor youth nor age,
> But, as it were, an after-dinner's sleep,
> Dreaming on both; for all thy blessed youth
> Become as aged, and doth beg the alms
> Of palsied eld; and when thou art old and rich,
> Thou hast neither heat, affection, limb, nor beauty,
> To make thy riches pleasant. What's yet in this
> That bears the name of life? Yet in this life
> Lie hid moe thousand deaths; yet death we fear,
> That makes these odds all even.
>
> (III. i. 5–41).

As these words linger in the calmed air, as Claudio submits, Isabella's voice is heard without, in unconscious denial of all this cerebral rejection, in a phrase as clear and welcome as life itself:

> What, ho! Peace here; grace and good company!

Isabella knows that she *cannot* do what Angelo demands and believes that her religious and honourable brother *cannot* ask her to do it, because he shares the same instincts that motivate her. But what she in fact does is to waken his hope and his fear again by letting him know that this one chance of life does after all exist. Her understanding of how men live or die, narrowed by her occluding rectitude, permits her to miscalculate Claudio's situation (although she shows enough appreciation of it to put the point before him with a good deal of nervous anxiety). After his first shock of dismay and anger against Angelo, he begs for life at the price of her honour. She turns upon him in understandable panic:

> O you beast!
> O faithless coward! O dishonest wretch!
> Wilt thou be made a man out of my vice?
> Is't not a kind of incest to take life
> From thine own sister's shame?   (III. i. 137–141)

Yet Isabella's miscalculation[1] ('What if she had been "clever" enough to keep away from Claudio altogether, thus ensuring that they both did their duty?') is, in the terms of the comedy, the happiest of mistakes. It enables the disguised Duke, who has placed himself to overhear the interview between brother and sister (the most terribly painful scene in any Shakespearian comedy), decisively to intervene in what has become a tragic impasse. So doing, he sets in train

[1] It is sometimes said that Isabella's reading of Claudio's mind here is justified because Claudio does after all towards the end of this scene grow resigned again. But he does so only because the Duke tells him that there really is no chance of life, that Angelo's offer was only a test of his sister's virtue. He accepts death only when there can be no appeal against the sentence.

the action which is finally to save them all after the manner of comedy.

From this point, and especially during the fourth Act, the play, with the Duke as its focus, alters a good deal in character. The trap for Angelo, entailing the 'bed-trick', has to be so elaborately devised and timed that we become more conscious of the complex arrangements for springing it than of anything else. The Duke tells all his aides, including Isabella, to get into their prepared positions, and they obey him without question. For Comedy, or Providence, has now taken charge. It is obvious that the Duke is not a realistic character in the same sense that the others are. (He has been interpreted as everything from an allegory of the Incarnate Lord to a portrait of King James I.) He seems, indeed, to duplicate in his own existence the antithetical patterns which we have observed at work elsewhere. We, and the characters in the play, can sometimes apprehend him as a real being, but sometimes the impulse prevails to see him as symbolic of a mysterious controlling power. He is able to keep providential control of the comedy only by being at the same time a part of the comedy. It was probably easier for the Renaissance than it is for us to see the wise ruler as the deputy of heaven. The mysterious dignity that seems to grow upon the Duke as the play proceeds does not mean more than the sharpening and focusing of this notion, until it emerges fully in Angelo's abject admission:

> O my dread lord,
> I should be guiltier than my guiltiness,
> To think I can be undiscernible,
> When I perceive your Grace, like pow'r divine,
> Hath look'd upon my passes.   (V. i. 364–8)

As a ruler of this kind, vicegerent of heaven, the Duke may almost be said to have a duty to look into his subjects' hearts. But that is the playwright's duty, too. It is not very difficult, for imaginative purposes, to apprehend the view, widespread in Shakespeare's time and vital to such plays as *Richard II* or *Henry V*, that a ruler could be both a man, with a man's individual weaknesses and inconsistencies, and also something more than man, the being whose special quality is emblematized in:

> the balm, the sceptre, and the ball,
> The sword, the mace, the crown imperial,
> The intertissued robe of gold and pearl. (*Henry V.*, IV. i. 256–8)

The Duke's real complexity emerges when this last status and function seem, as they often do in *Measure for Measure*, to be combined with yet others—those of the storyteller, or of Comedy itself. When the Duke withdraws from Vienna in order to put Angelo to the test, his action accords with his role as deputy of heaven, until we learn that after all he was fully informed about Angelo's entanglement with Mariana from the beginning; and then his action begins to look more consistent with that of a man who wishes to set off a story. When he tells Claudio that he must in any case die, or refrains from telling Isabella that Claudio is living still, it is foolish to blame him for cruelty, but proper to note that the reasons for his actions may include both power's prerogative to subject brother and sister to a final trial and the dramatist's need for a fine *dénouement* and a striking *coup de théâtre*. When he spares Barnardine, the condemned and dissolute felon in Claudio's prison, he does so as a merciful ruler who believes him unfit for death, and yet is at the same time acting as the guardian of comedy, by whose laws it would outrage us that any man (especially so vivid a one as Barnardine) should die. In all this, it is difficult to declare whether Shakespeare is saying that Providence is a kind of storyteller, or that a storyteller is a kind of Providence. We may feel the same agreeable doubts about Prospero in *The Tempest*, to whom the Duke is much akin. But Prospero is more plainly talking about *both* life and art in his speech at the end of the masque and in his 'Farewell'.

This is the quality of the fifth Act of *Measure for Measure*. It displays a self-conscious art of suspenseful narrative and simultaneously uses this to enforce the last test of Isabella and to resume the question about Mercy and Justice which was

Timon of Athens.

p. 2157

I TIMON OF ATHENS: the frontispiece to Rowe's edition, 1709.

II ALL'S WELL THAT ENDS WELL: a scene from Tyrone Guthrie's production
at the Shakespeare Memorial Theatre, Stratford-upon-Avon, 1959, *décor* by
Tanya Moiseiwitsch.　　　　　*(Angus McBean)*

John Piper: *Measure for Measure*

III MEASURE FOR MEASURE: from a design for the play by John Piper, reproduced by his kind permission.

IV TROILUS AND CRESSIDA: a scene from Tyrone Guthrie's production at the Old Vic, 1956, with designs by Frederick Crooke.

(Houston Rogers)

turned aside by Angelo's crime in the second Act. Angelo, like Bertram in *All's Well*, braves it out almost to the last, and apparently enjoys the earnest co-operation of the Duke in this. Half-way through the Act the entanglements are so dense that Mariana and Isabella, avouching the truth of the monstrous ransom and the subsequent 'bed-trick', have been made to look like conspirators against Angelo's patient virtue. The Duke puts them in his deputy's power, and leaves the stage, in order to return in his friar's disguise. The disguise of course is used (by being plucked off) to achieve a miraculous λύσις, that *sudden* untying of the knot so deeply approved by the theorists of neo-classical structure and of which Jonson was to prove himself in his three major comedies an even greater master than Shakespeare. Attention turns back to Angelo and to Isabella, now resuming their existences in that tragic and passionate air which was the atmosphere of the second and third Acts. Angelo's repentance is given far more emphasis than Bertram's, and is infinitely more convincing. It defines him for ever as one who has passed through tragic fires and will always bear their scars. His last words in the play are:

> I am sorry that such sorrow I procure;
> And so deep sticks it in my penitent heart
> That I crave death more willingly than mercy;
> 'Tis my deserving, and I do entreat it. (V.i. 472–5)

As for Isabella, she, too, is defined at last with a similar absence of ambiguity. Believing her brother to be dead and urged by Mariana to plead for the condemned Angelo, she hesitates at first; but Mariana's argument is too clear an echo of one that she herself had offered in the second Act:

> Isabel,
> Sweet Isabel, do yet but kneel by me;
> Hold up your hands, say nothing; I'll speak all.
> They say best men are moulded out of faults;
> And, for the most, become much more the better
> For being a little bad; so may my husband.
> O Isabel, will you not lend a knee? (V.i. 434–40)

Isabel's plea is, rightly and naturally in the circumstances, laconic and even a little chilly; but it is the gesture that matters, and Shakespeare did not make the mistake that Beaumont and Fletcher would have made of giving her a high-wrought, virtuoso declaration that would have slackened the suspension of our disbelief. In Isabella's plea, in the Duke's stern rejection of it, in his order for the production of Barnardine (whom he knows will be accompanied by the muffled Claudio), in his unmuffling of Claudio, and in his pardon to all, we have, as in majestic counterpoint, the operations of a merciful Providence patterned and enfolded with the delightful beneficences of Comedy. It is Isabella's special function to take part in this antiphon. This time Providence itself waits upon her forgiveness before it will act, while she is at the same time prepared for what seems, from the Duke's words, her obvious role as the heroine of a comedy that ends in her marriage, as comedies ought to end. In all this blaze of ordered joy, the identity of these two personages shifts between the real and the symbolic, just as the words from the Sermon on the Mount are both a theophany and the outline of a tale that ends with happiness:

> Be ye therefore merciful, as your Father also is merciful.
> Judge not, and ye shall not be judged: condemn not, and ye shall not be condemned: forgive, and ye shall be forgiven.
> Give and it shall be given unto you: a good measure, pressed down, shaken together, and running over shall men give unto your bosom: for with what measure ye mete, with the same shall men mete to you again.

IV

TROILUS AND CRESSIDA

Sir Walter Greg called *Troilus and Cressida* 'a play of puzzles'. Its classification was long disputed, though we now call it a 'tragical satire'. Its diction is often obscure; its love-poetry is passionate and intellectually tough in Donne's manner. It differs from Shakespeare's earlier plays by its special stress on staged debates between characters, and by the absence of a single major character on whom our imagination may fasten (instead, there is an exceptionally large number of important speaking parts). Ideas and attitudes are kept in constant movement throughout it; there are many speeches which openly acknowledge their allegiance to rhetorical disciplines and at the same time transcend them with a richness of figure and feeling that seems very personal to Shakespeare, and here encompasses an element of bitter bawdry which for some readers colours the whole play. Peter Alexander's theory that it was specially written for an Inns of Court audience has been generally approved. A crowd of young barristers and their guests would probably have enjoyed more than the popular audience at the Globe would the obliquity of the play, its occasional legal jokes, and its angry, metaphysical and highbrow temper.

Although Shakespeare took his title from the love-story, the war-story is just as important. The two themes of love and war, which are handled with such plangent nobility in Othello's dedication of himself and all his romantic history to his 'fair warrior' and which for so long had been a literary archetype, here suffer their traditional equilibrium to become a 'torture', in the words of John Crowe Ransom's poem:

> At length I saw these lovers fully were come
> Into their torture of equilibrium.

The themes, as Theodore Spencer said, are 'interwoven in a deliberate and elaborate pattern'; Thersites's crude summary of them 'Lechery, lechery; still wars and lechery; nothing else holds fashion' is not the last word about them or about the experience of Troilus and Cressida, and although the play is difficult to classify, its writing and planning give no impression that Shakespeare was half-hearted or inattentive.

It is a mistake to exaggerate the sardonic nature of Shakespeare's treatment of the war-story by comparing it directly with the *Iliad*. The Homeric tale had long been modified by the medieval bias in favour of the Trojans and by the habit of thinking of the Greeks as grossly unchivalric. Many European countries traced their ancestry back to the Trojans (Holinshed, Shakespeare's great source-book for English history, was misinforming his readers in Shakespeare's own time that the name 'Britain' derived from Aeneas's grandson Brutus). There was a large body of pseudo-historical writing about the war, which was regarded as having as much or greater authority than Homer. Shakespeare's principal source was Caxton's ever-popular *Recuyell* (or 'collection') *of the Historyes of Troye* (1475), a work which ultimately derives from a twelfth-century French composition that claims to know more history than Homer. From the same ultimate source came Lydgate's *Troy Book*, which many believe was also used by Shakespeare. Shakespeare probably did not read the *Iliad* in Greek, but when his play was written (*c.* 1602) some instalments (Books i, ii, and vii to ix) of the first English translation by George Chapman had appeared, and it is more than likely that Shakespeare did not neglect Chapman's defiantly epoch-making enterprise. He would have found in it, for example, the character of Thersites, who is unknown to Caxton or Lydgate.

Although it has been doubted, it is also very probable that he knew the two great preceding treatments of the love-story, Chaucer's *Troilus and Criseyde* and Robert Henryson's *Testament of Cresseid*. The latter would have been available to him in editions of Chaucer which print Henryson's fine poem as a sequel. It takes a much more mordant view than Chaucer did, and by Shakespeare's time this had become traditional: Cressida is the prototype of the fickle wanton, Pandarus of the vile go-between, and Troilus of the faithful, cheated lover. Shakespeare shows himself very conscious of their eponymous roles, as in Pandarus's declaration:

If ever you prove false one to another, since I have taken such pains
to bring you together, let all pitiful goers-between be call'd to the
world's end after my name—call them all Pandars; let all constant
men be Troiluses, all false women Cressidas, and all brokers between
Pandars. Say 'Amen'.

Thus, while Shakespeare's treatment of Troilus remains
relatively the same as Chaucer's, he is much less kindly to the
other two, although it is true that Pandarus is a comic
bustler, who is certainly not scourged from our sympathy
after the manner of Jonsonian satire; whose final dis-
appointment, therefore, is not a matter for self-righteous
pleasure, but saddens us a little. Chaucer was writing within
the tradition of courtly love, which had now been supplanted by that of Christian marriage. As is common
within that latter tradition, Shakespeare tends to gloss over
the man's share in the mutual breach of prescribed sexual
ethics, while making it plain that the lovers consummated
their betrothal pledge without benefit of priest.[1]

The sardonic nature of Shakespeare's rendering of both
these ancient, famous stories, as well as his practice of interweaving them, are clearly announced in the play's first few
minutes. The 'armed' Prologue, in curiously mannered and
almost Miltonic diction, sounds loud with brass and the rattle
of armament:

> Now on Dardan plains
> The fresh and yet unbruised Greeks do pitch
> Their brave pavilions: Priam's six-gated city,
> Dardan, and Tymbria, Helias, Chetas, Troien,
> And Antenorides, with massy staples
> And corresponsive and fulfilling bolts,
> Sperr up the sons of Troy.
> Now expectation, tickling skittish spirits
> On one and other side, Troyan and Greek,
> Sets all on hazard.

This slightly self-deriding exercise in onomatopoeia is a

---

[1] On the sources see especially Alice Walker's New Cambridge edition
(1957), and K. Muir, *Shakespeare's Sources I* (1957), 78–96.

splendidly discordant version of that other Prologue to
famous victories in *Henry V*. It is followed by a scene which
strikes sharply across it with another discord. The rousing
fights for which the Prologue tickles expectation do not
occur. Instead, there enters the sick-hearted Troilus, not
arming but unarming:

> Call here my varlet; I'll unarm again:
> Why should I war without the walls of Troy
> That find such cruel battle here within?

This is one of those juxtapositions which Shakespeare made
into a high art of dramatic contrast, especially in this play.
Pandarus, who has been at work for some time as go-
between, leaves in a huff because Troilus won't be patient
(the lover woos the pandar, another ironic inversion), and by
the end of the first scene the clangorous Prologue appears
shrill and diminished. The second scene makes more of this.
It introduces Cressida: a bold, witty, courtly person
thoroughly able to manage Pandarus. Their conversation reveals that Cressida's consent is a foregone conclusion (and
this throws an ironical jest back at Troilus's agonies and
frustrations) and depicts the Trojan world as an urbane
civilization which does not take itself too seriously.

    When we turn in the next scene (I.iii) to war, politics, and
the Greeks, we find a people, or, rather, a beleaguered army,
which does take its situation much more gravely. This is the
first of the two great debate-scenes. It is not too much to
say that the Greek debate and what follows it, and the
Trojan debate in II.ii, are the keys to the meaning and con-
struction of the entire play. In the Greek debate we meet all
at once the major Homeric personages except Achilles and
Ajax, who are both present by implication: for all the
debaters have Achilles's insubordination and Ajax's pride in
mind. In the bristly and rather empty rhetoric of
Agamemnon's exordium the tone of the armed Prologue
recurs. Of Ulysses's two long speeches, the first (ll. 54-137),
the famous speech on 'degree' (= 'rank', social order viewed

as the mirror of cosmic order), exposes the principle by
which an army and a campaign ought to be run; the second
(ll. 141–84) gives a vivid account of how Achilles is causing
chaos by disregarding what is due to rank. The Greeks have
just exhausted this theme (but seem to have no plan for
remedial action) when Aeneas arrives as herald to deliver
Hector's challenge to single combat: a challenge of a purely
chivalric-medieval kind in which the knights are to pledge
the beauty and honour of their ladies. Greek and Trojan are
here distinguished as blunt or ceremonious. At first
Agamemnon simply cannot understand Aeneas's courtly
rendering of 'Which of you is Agamemnon?':

> *Aen.*   How may
> A stranger to those most imperial looks
> Know them from eyes of other mortals?
> *Agam.* How?
> *Aen.* Ay;
> I ask, that I might waken reverence,
> And bid the cheek be ready with a blush
> Modest as Morning when she coldly eyes
> The youthful Phoebus.
> Which is that god in office, guiding men?
> Which is the high and mighty Agamemnon?
> *Agam.* This Troyan scorns us, or the men of Troy
> Are ceremonious courtiers.   (I. iii. 223–34)

Such a passage makes fun of the difference between the
two sides, but does not espouse either. When the Greeks
accept the challenge, they also accept Ulysses's plan for using
it as a means of bringing Achilles back into the war: the
boastful Ajax is to be treated as though he were the Greeks'
best man and elected challenger; if he loses, there's no great
harm done, since the Greek army can spare him; but if he
wins, then Achilles will feel that his reputation is in deadly
danger and will, they hope, arm for battle again. Most of the
rest of the Achilles-story in the play revolves round this
simple scheme.

Because Ulysses unfolds the theme of 'degree' with the

magnification proper to an orator addressing a council of war, amplifying it with the macrocosmic analogy, the speech has often been extrapolated as a statement of the Shakespearian or Elizabethan world-view. It may be so; but if we keep it in its dramatic context, we perceive that there is a sardonic contrast between Ulysses's insistence on rank and his subsequent plan to invert, for politico-military ends, the due precedence of Achilles over Ajax. By manipulating Ajax's conceit against Achilles's pride, putting the weak above the head of the strong, the Greeks hope to enforce proper order again. This is a politic game, the art of the possible, and it defines the 'degree' speech, with some irony, as the rhetoric of an ideal. Furthermore, the ingenious scheme is opportunist in character: Aeneas's quite unexpected challenge, not anything decided by a debate which seemed to be getting nowhere, gave Ulysses the idea for it. And, although it is elaborately maintained up to the fifth Act and looks almost like succeeding, nothing comes of it in the end. Achilles suddenly withdraws from the combat for a remarkably trivial and vague reason (V. i. 35ff), and when he does finally fight it is for a quite different cause: to revenge Patroclus's death on Hector. Thus the huge structure built on the Greek debate-scene is deliberately left roofless; Ulysses the master-politician and tireless orator has affairs jerked from his hands and is left darkling.

The issue before the Trojans in *their* debate-scene (II.ii) is not how to continue the war but whether to continue it. This is the strangest scene in the play and has caused much dispute. The debate is much more of a genuine debate than the Greek one; Shakespeare seems determined to keep our sympathies swaying back and forth between the appeal to reason (Hector's) and that to passion (Troilus's). Because he is uncertain of the future and thinks that the lives squandered in Helen's cause are worth more than she is, Hector advises peace. Troilus bursts out that Priam's honour, which depends upon keeping Helen, is not to be measured by Hector's fears and reasons, and when the priest Helenus rebukes him for

this he merely taunts him for being a coward. There is something romantic and absolute about Troilus's youthful fervour
here and elsewhere which is very attractive to a part of our
minds. The debate then goes deeper. Troilus and Hector
begin to discuss whether they ought to be motivated by the
value of Helen in herself, or by the value they have put upon
her in the past by committing themselves to fighting for her.
Both seem to agree that in herself Helen is not worth much,
and Hector wants the Trojans simply to remember this; it is
madness to continue to value an object simply because it was
once thought a prize worth having. Troilus replies with an
analogy: a man chooses a wife, a matter in which both 'will'
(= 'passion') and judgement are involved, and therefore a
very delicate choice. But the choice once made is irrevocable,
if the man is to 'stand firm by honour'. So the Trojans,
thinking her valuable, stole Helen; now they are distasted
with her. But if they are to avoid inconsistency, cowardice,
and dishonour, they can no more give her up than a man can
give up the wife whom he has grown to dislike. Cassandra
now makes her first entrance, and, after her prophecy of
doom, Hector asks Troilus whether the thought that Troy
may be conquered makes any difference. Troilus faces up to
this: the rightness of a course is not affected by whether it
succeeds or not:

> Why, brother Hector,
> We may not think the justness of each act
> Such and no other than event doth form it.   (II.ii. 118–20)

Paris seconds him, with different arguments. Troilus had
argued that the original rape of Helen was a just act of
revenge (for the Greeks' rape of Priam's sister, Hesione);
Paris claims that, if the rape of Helen was a crime, the dis-
grace can be wiped off by 'honourable keeping her'. Hector's
reply to all this, an appeal to the law of nature and of
nations, is unanswerable on its own level. His argument is a
very Elizabethan one and would perhaps have seemed wholly
persuasive to an Elizabethan audience. It is all very well, he

says, to talk about what we owe ourselves in honour, but the plain fact is that Helen is Menelaus's wife and the Trojans have no right to her:

> If Helen, then, be wife to Sparta's king—
> As it is known she is—these moral laws
> Of nature and of nations speak aloud
> To have her back return'd. Thus to persist
> In doing wrong extenuates not wrong,
> But makes it much more heavy.　　(II. ii. 183–8)

Hector's next step, his sudden retraction, is the most puzzling incident in the play:

> Hector's opinion
> Is this, in way of truth. Yet, ne'er the less,
> My spritely brethren, I propend to you
> In resolution to keep Helen still;
> For 'tis a cause that hath no mean dependence
> Upon our joint and several dignities.　　(II. ii. 188–93)

Probably the 'explanation' for it is simply that otherwise the play would have had to stop. This is an explanation that supplies a motive which Hector himself could hardly have recognized, and is therefore unsatisfactory from the point of view of consistent characterization; but that is not the only criterion in a work of dramatic art.

The Trojan decision is fatal to them. For the rest of the play Hector relapses into the noble, doomed warrior of tradition. But Troilus remains consistent with the self which he had exposed in the debate, which therefore continues to reverberate during the rest of both the war-action and the love-action. His notion that honour resides in a man's not ratting on his own choice is carefully contrasted with the Achillean notion, which is deliberately aggravated by Ulysses for his politic purposes in his great speech on the subject (III.iii. 145-90), that honour is what is given to you by other people and is therefore ruled by time and chance. It was precisely this notion of honour as 'opinion', an out-ward thing measured by other men's judgements and the

vulgar fancies of the fickle mob, which was passionately
repudiated by Chapman and many other Elizabethan writers
when they tried to discern what greatness really is. Ulysses,
however, vividly states the facts of political life and not the
austere longings of Elizabethan neo-Stoicism. Achilles's con-
sequent alarm at the state of his reputation is at once a re-
sponse to those facts, for which he cannot be blamed, and a
designed contrast with Troilus's passionate commitment to
the view that time and fortune cannot modify original
virtue.

This commitment is of a piece with his deception by
Cressida and his total pledge to her. In a world which contains the Ulyssean facts (that women are fickle and that
reputations fade), Shakespeare shows both the glorious and
the self-destructive character of Troilus's absoluteness, his
truth to himself. With his glory and his fault locked together
in him, Troilus very closely resembles Othello, and is a tragic
hero.

The scene (III.ii) in which the lovers finally come together
is treated by Shakespeare as the birth of a legend, but is not
to be taken simply as a satirical version of it. Troilus's
feelings are too genuine for that. There is no doubt that
Theodore Spencer is right as against O. J. Campbell when he
says that Troilus's love is both sensual *and* idealistic. He has
placed, to the accompaniment of some hard-breathing desire,
an ideal valuation on the false Cressid, and to this he clings
for ever. She can respond seriously for the time being, and
continues to do so later on in the three continuous scenes
(IV.ii-iv) which deal with their parting. Campbell's view
that they are both depicted as a couple of sated sensualists is
quite unacceptable and derives from his determination to
make the whole play conform to the satirical mode. It is a
much more subtle play than Thersites thinks. At the first
news that Cressida must go to the Greek camp, Troilus is
shocked into silence and simplicity; her grief contains no
hint that she is merely behaving. But she knows little of herself, of the time-directed nature of her truth, as her indigna-

tion at Troilus's plea to her to be true reveals. Time is the enemy of all lovers, and both the constant and the fickle are here seen beneath that climbing shadow, which puts satire far from us as we contemplate them in these scenes.

This shadow is removed from Cressida when her unstable and fickle nature is revealed in IV.v. Passively she allows herself to be carried on the tide of events, somewhat in the manner of Chaucer's heroine. The two speeches by Ulysses in this scene, one about Cressida, the other about Troilus, make it plain that the Helen-situation, as examined in the Trojan debate, is being repeated in the relation of Troilus to Cressida. The object to which Troilus attaches such value is shown *by time* to be valueless. Once it was not so, just as once, for Troilus, Helen was a true prize and a just deed. But 'once' for Troilus is 'always', as the debate showed. This is the source of his agony in the last of the love-story scenes (V.ii) where Troilus watches Cressida's wanton invitation to Diomed. His speech is a complete confusion between the value he once put upon Cressida and what she now appears by 'ocular proof' to be. His commitment to what she was makes it impossible for him to accept what she is. This is Troilus's peculiarly personal fate, or punishment:

> This she? No; this is Diomed's Cressida.
> If beauty have a soul, this is not she;
> If souls guide vows, if vows be sanctimonies,
> If sanctimony be the gods' delight,
> If there be rule in unity itself,
> This was not she. O madness of discourse,
> That cause sets up with and against itself!
> Bifold authority! where reason can revolt
> Without perdition, and loss assume all reason
> Without revolt: this is, and is not, Cressid.   (V. ii. 135-44)

Although the speech ends with a cluster of the food-and-taste images frequent in this play, revealing Troilus's apprehension of grossness in the valued object, he can no more give up his love than he could accept Hector's argument that things are what they are, and that losses ought to be cut.

During the rest of the play Troilus is mastered by his passionate consistency, vows revenge on Diomed, proclaims his love, and urges to the fight with reckless courage. The 'worthless' cause for which he fights is Cressida's now as well as Helen's.

Shakespeare does not suggest that we should withhold our admiration and pity for this; but in what remains of the war-story he does suggest, Ulysses-like, that Troilus is out of accord with the facts of the Trojan war and is likely to come to grief. The finale of the play strengthens the sardonic treatment of hopes and ideals which is the air that Thersites, Ulysses, and Diomed breathe, and which Troilus is none the worse for finding stifling. He does not get his revenge, and to him is allotted the penultimate speech, which the audience knows is false prophecy about how the war will really end. When Hector is slain by Achilles the incident is deliberately made a far seamier affair than it was in Shakespeare's source—the opportunist murder of an unarmed man by a troop of soldiers.

The death of Hector is just sufficiently decisive to give the play an ending, but is in a minor key of melancholy. Shakespeare's sophisticated treatment of the whole story, in which elaborate schemes run to waste (those of Pandarus as well as Ulysses) and paths of motivation peter out in the jungle of accident, is sufficiently pointed by this conclusion in which nothing is concluded, except in the audience's foreknowledge. This wonderfully composed and highly-wrought work is thus sharply bent towards the satirical and the off-beat, and is darkened throughout with Thersites's savage, ineffectual commentary. But Shakespeare was not content to accept the tale of Troy only as a sardonic amusement, a way of cutting ancient heroes down to size. In the heart of all its accomplished inversions and achieved rhetoric, its diminishing commentary and its squalid opportunism, denied by them and yet given in our imaginations real power to deny them, lies what was in such a context the most difficult, because the most simple, artefact

of all: the simply constant Troilus, who might well have
borrowed Parolles's astounding line: 'Simply the thing I
am shall make me live':

> Alas,
> I am as true as truth's simplicity
> And simpler than the infancy of truth.

V

TIMON OF ATHENS

Compared with the three other plays considered here, *Timon*
is a slight structure. Although it is only the sixth shortest
of Shakespeare's plays and could not have required much
more than tidying up, the text we have probably represents an
incomplete draft, and there is no evidence that it was ever
performed in Shakespeare's time. Timon's story had long
been a stock example of extreme misanthropy.[1] Shakespeare
certainly knew Plutarch's brief, almost anecdotal, digression
on Timon in his *Life of Antony* (in Sir Thomas North's
translation), and it seems probable that he knew Lucian's
dialogue *Timon* (available in Latin, French, and Italian
versions), which has a pattern corresponding to Shakespeare's
play. The gods decide to restore the fortunes of Timon, a
fallen prodigal, and, digging, he finds a mass of golden
treasure. But when his false friends seek him out again, they
are driven off with blows of his pick, the last being
Thrasycles, a hypocritical philosopher (Shakespeare took
his name, Apemantus, for the corresponding character from
Plutarch). There are other conjectural sources of which the
most important is *Timon*, an anonymous school or university play perhaps dating from about 1600. Shakespeare
designed his play very clearly in two related parts. The
first three Acts tell the story of his ruin and disillusionment,

---

[1] See W. Farnham, *Shakespeare's Tragic Frontier* (1950), pp. 50–67.

the last two show Timon fixed in settled hatred of the world, until death comes and he leaves it to Alcibiades to deal with his enemies and lament his passing. Alcibiades's story counterpoints Timon's. He is shown as the victim of Athenian ingratitude, and eventually returns to purge the corrupted city. Two other lesser characters have a continuous but contrasting relationship with Timon: Apemantus the philosopher, and Flavius, Timon's faithful steward.

There have been very conflicting interpretations of the central personage. He has been seen in the first half of the play as a godlike image of perfect friendship, a universal or supreme lover, of boundless, unjudging charity, finding 'complete satisfaction in the inter-communion of heart with heart, and gift with gift'.[1] Others claim that Timon is set before us only as an object of satire, illustrating the old adage that a fool and his money are soon parted. This latitude of interpretation may partly be due to Timon's not being very strongly individuated, despite all that he is given to say. Spareness in characterization accompanied by an absence of complexity in the action have readily suggested also that Shakespeare was less than usually concerned with ordinary theatrical effectiveness and more with extrapolating a moral idea. From this it is a short step to the conclusion that *Timon* was intended to be a dramatized parable or morality-play and that basically its characters allegorize virtues and vices: 'it is the medieval morality play, only so much altered as to bring it very near to perfection.'[2] Yet others maintain (and in my view they are right) that Shakespeare probably set out to create a tragic hero having something in common with Lear and Othello, and that he failed to do so partly because he had not chosen a story and theme capable of sustaining him.

The play opens with great brilliance in Timon's house in Athens. It is a typical morning in Timon's life of bounty,

[1] G. Wilson Knight, *The Wheel of Fire* (1949 edn.), p. 212.

[2] A. S. Collins 'Timon of Athens: a Reconsideration', *R.E.S.*, XXII (1946), 98.

but it is also one that foreshadows his imminent ruin. The Poet and the Painter, the Jeweller and the Merchant, who throng to him with their gifts, are a little too cheaply and obviously doing well at Timon's expense. These characters, with their self-conscious jargon, lofty airs, and excessive courtesy to one another, are comic sketches which show that Shakespeare had observed, with an amused and pene-trating eye, the 'small poets' and pretentious *salons* of his, and other, times. Although he is unaware of it himself, the Poet (who describes his allegorical verses about the man who, deserted by Fortune, is then abandoned by his friends) evokes an obvious analogy for the benefit of the audience. When Timon enters, we see him first settling the debts of an imprisoned friend and then enabling a servant to marry the daughter of a rich, mean Athenian, who consents to the match only when Timon undertakes to double the dowry. There is no criticism of Timon's generosity here, but he seems unable to accept gifts from others without giving in return more richly still. In the next scene there is pro-digality in his refusal to accept the return of the sum which he had sent to the debtor (who has suddenly inherited vast wealth); in the way in which his talk of friendship is always interwoven with the handing out of presents; and in such a sudden impulse as this:

> And now I remember, my lord, you gave good words the other day of a bay courser I rode on. 'Tis yours because you lik'd it.

An unduly constricted view of human behaviour is implied in Timon's 'I know no man / Can justly praise but what he does affect' (I.ii. 212–3). So far from there being a sense of 'inter-communion', even in his own house Timon seems strangely isolated amidst the crowds as he participates in these rather schematic events: no *friends* are really visible— though Timon constantly uses the word of those who so assiduously 'lord Timon' him—no wife, no companion.

Two other characters, Apemantus and Flavius, provide

an instructive commentary. Apemantus, over-proud that he flatters no man, acts as a warning voice:

> O you gods, what a number of men eats Timon, and he sees 'em not! It grieves me to see so many dip their meat in one man's blood; and all the madness is, he cheers them up too.

(I. ii. 36–41)

Despite his own dislikeable nature, Apemantus helps to re-define those whom Timon so freely calls his *friends* as *flatterers*, and to bring home to the audience a moral point with which they would be extremely familiar (one, indeed, on which Plutarch had written at great length), namely, that it is very hard to discern the one from the other:

> a man shall never see flatterers so much as approach unto such persons as are in decay, whose state is cracked and credit waxeth cool; but look where there is the glory of the world, where there is authority and power, thither they flock, and there they grow: no sooner is there a change of fortune but they sneak and slink away, and are no more seen. [1]

The method for resisting flatterers was to *know thyself*. Flavius, the faithful steward, is the witness that Timon does not know himself in respect of his most relevant property and emblem, his purse. It is Flavius who countervails all the bustle of present-giving and talk of friends and bounty by revealing that Timon is already ruined:

> What will this come to?
> He commands us to provide and give great gifts,
> And all out of an empty coffer;
> Nor will he know his purse, or yield me this,
> To show him what a beggar his heart is,
> Being of no power to make his wishes good. (I.ii. 188–93)

Timon, then, has for some time been refusing to face facts. He has been living like Dryden's Mark Antony, 'in a golden dream of love and friendship', and when Flavius finally manages in the second Act to thrust the facts under

[1] Plutarch, 'How a Man may Discern a Flatterer from a Friend', *Moralia* (Everyman edn., 1912), p. 39.

his nose, at a point in the play after we have already seen his creditors beginning to take action for the recovery of their money, he finds it very hard to believe that he is poor. His bemused line 'To Lacedaemon did my land extend' marvellously conveys the bewilderment of a man awaking from a dream. It is now that he admits 'Unwisely, not ignobly, have I given', while Flavius weeps in distress.

Timon has a harsher awakening yet. It is not he but the commercial world of Athens—as bad a place as Volpone's Venice—that comes under the lash in the three brilliantly varied and horrid scenes of the third Act, which show what happens when Timon's flatterers are asked to help him out. As Una Ellis-Fermor wrote:

> The masterly skill of long experience lies behind the treatment of the parallel episodes of Lucullus, Lucius, Sempronius, and Ventidius, so handled, in different ways, as to avoid repetition while building up the impression of accumulation, to reveal at once the individuality of characters and the monotony of their behaviour. No dramatic novice wrote this. [1]

Timon's messengers are sent empty away, and he reacts not now with bewilderment but with rage. The scene (III.iv) in which he is surrounded, like a baited animal, by a pack of howling creditors is a dreadful parodic counter-part of the earlier scenes in which he was surrounded by a crowd of mock-diffident beneficiaries. The same cal-culated balance may be observed in the relation of the second banquet-scene (III.vi) to the first (I.ii). The elegant food that gratified the four senses (I.ii. 121) has become lukewarm water and stones, the friends are changed into beasts, the host's speech of welcome into a long commination (III.vi. 88–104). Timon stage-manages the revelation of how his own nature has itself been transformed from sweetness and dreamy abundance into bitterness and withdrawal as though he were the *régisseur* of some desperate anti-masque, fitly opposite to the masque of Cupid performed

---

[1] *Shakespeare the Dramatist* (1961), p. 167.

at that earlier feast. He still gives and gives out, but what he gives are stones, projected from him in hurling movements of fury.

Up to this point the play has been marked by that controlled forward movement of event and character which is so characteristic of Shakespeare's and of most successful dramatic art. It is easy to believe that Timon's trust in his friends, built as it is on complete unawareness about them, should, when washed by so icy a wave of reality, corrode into violent repugnance. The very obviousness of the moral paradigm helps us to believe that so, indeed, did it happen. It is not suggested in this part of the play that the pattern of experience which has befallen Timon is uniquely strange and never before traced out. There are, as the Painter observes, 'A thousand moral paintings . . . That shall demonstrate these quick blows of Fortune's'; the comments of Apemantus ('Thus honest fools lay out their wealth on curtsies'), the ironically unaware reflections of Timon himself ('what need we have any friends, if we should ne'er have need of them?'), the First Stranger's remarks about Lucius ('Why, this is the world's soul: and just of the same piece / Is every flatterer's spirit')—these all help to generalize the meaning of the events and relate them to the thousand moral treatises on ingratitude and prodigality and flattery. The sense that Timon's experience illustrates a general truth, while it need not detract from the sharpness of his own lessoning, is precisely that quality which gives the play its character of a moral apologue. All the commentators have recognized that character, even though they may not all wish to see it simply as a medieval morality Shakespearianized.

But in the last two Acts of the play both the credibilizing generalization of the theme and the forward-moving motivation of the protagonist are almost completely checked. For the whole point about Timon is that he now becomes unique, strange, the archetype of his kind, the famous Misanthrope: 'I am Misanthropos, and hate mankind.' The only change that does occur is the enlargement of his hatred to include the whole cosmic process. The extraordinary inclusiveness of his condemnation of all human and animal life and of all Nature is a thing for wonder and dismay. We contemplate him with amazement because he goes so far; but after a while the amazement palls, just as the magnified creatures of Dryden's heroic plays—'as far above the ordinary proportion of the stage, as that is beyond the words and actions of common life'—at first may make us gasp and stretch our eyes, but later begin to languish before our desire that they should do more than just parade their excess. For the complement to Timon's uniqueness is his unchangeability. Movement within him ceases, and he becomes fixed for much of the rest of the play in an eternal gesture of repugnance as though his last banquet had been like that mythological one at which the guests were turned to stone.

Timon's speeches in the last two Acts contain some very great poetry (though much of it is only doubtfully *dramatic* poetry) which reminds all their readers of the terrible curses and invocations of Lear. His situation, driven out into the wilderness by ingratitude, is very like Lear's. But Lear's vision of the great world wearing out to naught is one which, in Keats's words, he 'burns through'. As he opens his mind at length to the truth about himself, pain alters to insight, and he is able to overcome the poisons of ingratitude and the desire to punish. This never happens to Timon. The poisons blacken all his vision, even though his enemies are commoner and smaller than Lear's. The faithful love of his steward is treated by him (IV.iii) only as a grudgingly received exception to his obsessional rule that all men are contemptible. 'One might express the difference between Lear and Timon by saying that Lear in affliction comes to *see* as he never did before; Timon does not undergo the ultimate ordeal of madness and the utmost he attains is to *see through* particular shams and injustices.' [1]

In the end Timon's tone grows tedious. His voice seeks again and again the same pitch of bitter fury. The long

[1] J. C. Maxwell, New Cambridge ed. (1957), p. xxxvii.

speeches, which as isolated curses or poems of hatred are
charged with some of Shakespeare's most effective and
resonant images, oppress the imagination. We soon realize
that the face Timon presents to his visitors, who come to
watch him prowling up and down in the cage of his hatred,
will always be the same; he seems to have passed beyond that
ability to be modified by his experience which is the continuing life of a dramatic character. It is a blessed relief when,
with the approach of death, invective gives way to elegy,
in lines of grave and bitter beauty unsurpassed in Shakes-
speare:

> I have a tree, which grows here in my close,
> That mine own use invites me to cut down,
> And shortly must I fell it. Tell my friends,
> Tell Athens, in the sequence of degree
> From high to low throughout, that whoso please
> To stop affliction, let him take his haste,
> Come hither ere my tree hath felt the axe,
> And hang himself. I pray you do my greeting . . .
>
> Come not to me again; but say to Athens,
> Timon hath made his everlasting mansion
> Upon the beached verge of the salt flood,
> Who once a day with his embossed froth
> The turbulent surge shall cover. Thither come,
> And let my grave-stone be your oracle.
> Lips, let four words go by and language end:
> What is amiss, plague and infection mend!
> Graves only be men's works, and death their gain!
> Sun, hide thy beams; Timon hath done his reign.
>
> (V. i. 203-21). [1]

When, later, in the Senate of a yielding and contrite city
Alcibiades reads Timon's furious epitaph on himself, what
Alicibiades says and does makes it clear enough that Timon's
misanthropy is no statement of the poet's own judgement
on the world. The state can still be purged of breathless
wrong and pursy insolence; there is still the faithful steward;

[1] This quotation follows the readings of the New Cambridge text.

and even if men forbid themselves tenderness, then Nature
herself will supply the recompense:

> Though thou abhorr'dst in us our human griefs,
> Scornd'st our brain's flow, and those our droplets which
> From niggard nature fall, yet rich conceit
> Taught thee to make vast Neptune weep for aye
> On thy low grave, on faults forgiven.

VI

CONCLUSION

The nature of Shakespeare's art in the problem plays entailed
suspensions of judgement and multiple loose ends, intellec-
tual promptings that are diverted by story, and characters
who show their awareness of their own fictive nature. For
these and other reasons it is easy to read into these plays what
we wish to find there, and to substitute our more common-
place symmetries for Shakespeare's subtler ones. It is also
easy to accuse Shakespeare of partial failure, perhaps because
there is a genuine element of miscalculation, perhaps
because we cannot read his clues. If we want to say that
Timon of Athens is unsatisfying primarily because his instinct
for choosing the 'right' source and subject seems for once to
have failed him, the reasons for failure, if it is admitted, in
All's Well are different: he missed opportunities which his
story seemed to provide. As Shakespeare's experiments they
are of course more instructive than the successes of lesser
men, especially since he was at the height of his poetic powers
when he wrote them. The powers and the experimentation
are both seen in the other two plays. *Measure for Measure* is
the beneficiary of the lessons learnt in the making of *All's
Well* (as *Lear* may well be of *Timon*) and is one of the most
subtle and testing expressions of his genius. *Troilus and
Cressida* is a play which has no real counterpart elsewhere in

his work, but, in finding its own somewhat less exacting form, achieves a success which can only be described as brilliant—brilliant in its rhetoric, in its flashing and blazing contrasts of character and of subject, and in its glittering design.

WILLIAM SHAKESPEARE

THE PROBLEM PLAYS

Troilus and Cressida · All's Well That Ends Well

Measure for Measure · Timon of Athens

A SELECT BIBLIOGRAPHY

(Books published in London, unless stated otherwise)

Full bibliographical descriptions of the separate quarto editions and of the first collected edition of *Mr. William Shakespeare's Comedies, Histories, & Tragedies*, 1623 (the FIRST FOLIO) are given in W. W. Greg, *A Bibliography of the English Printed Drama to the Restoration*, 4 vols. 1940–59.

ABBREVIATIONS

EC:	*Essays in Criticism*
ELH:	*English Literary History*
ES:	*English Studies*
HLQ:	*Huntington Library Quarterly*
JEGP:	*Journal of English and Germanic Philology*
MLR:	*Modern Language Review*
PMLA:	*Publications of the Modern Language Association*
RES:	*Review of English Studies*
ShJ:	*Shakespeare Jahrbuch*
ShQ:	*Shakespeare Quarterly*
ShS:	*Shakespeare Survey*

GENERAL CRITICISM

CHAMBERS, Sir E. K. *William Shakespeare: A Study of Facts and Problems*, Vol. I. Oxford, 1930.

LAWRENCE, W. W. *Shakespeare's Problem Comedies*. New York, 1931.

CHARLTON, H. B. *Shakespearian Comedy*. 1938

CAMPBELL, O. J. *Shakespeare's Satire*. New York, 1943.

PARROTT, T. M. *Shakespearian Comedy*. Oxford, 1949.

TILLYARD, E. M. W. *Shakespeare's Problem Plays*. 1950.

BRADBROOK, M. C. *Shakespeare and Elizabethan Poetry*. 1951.

——*The Growth and Structure of Elizabethan Comedy*. 1955.

BROWN, J. R. *Shakespeare and his Comedies.* 1957.

MUIR, K. *Shakespeare's Sources*, Vol. 1. 1957.

BULLOUGH, G. *Narrative and Dramatic Sources of Shakespeare*, Vol. II. 1958.

EVANS, B. *Shakespeare's Comedies.* Oxford, 1960.

TROILUS AND CRESSIDA

First edition: The Historie of Troylus and Cresseida. As it was acted by the Kings Maiesties servants at the Globe. Written by William Shakespeare. . . 1609. Reprinted in the FIRST FOLIO.

Modern editions: Arden ed. Deighton (1906); Tudor, ed. Tatlock (1912); Yale, ed. Paradise (1927); Warwick, ed. Dobrée (1938); New Variorum, ed. Hillebrand and Baldwin (1953); New Cambridge, ed. Walker (1957).

CRITICAL STUDIES

SMALL, R. A. *The Stage-quarrel between Ben Jonson and the so-called Poetasters*, Breslau, 1899.

TATLOCK, J. S. P. 'The Siege of Troy in Elizabethan Literature, especially in Shakespeare and Heywood.' *PMLA*, XXX, 1915, 673–770.

ROLLINS, H. E. 'The Troilus-Cressida Story from Chaucer to Shakespeare.' *PMLA*, XXXII, 1917, 383–429.

ALEXANDER, P, 'Troilus and Cressida, 1609.' *Library*, IX, 1928, 267–86.

KNIGHT, G. W. 'The Philosophy of *Troilus and Cressida*', in *The Wheel of Fire*. 1930, 1947.

SPENCER, T. 'A Commentary on Shakespeare's *Troilus and Cressida*.' *Studies in English Literature*, Tokyo, XVI, 1936, 1–42.

CAMPBELL, O. J. *Comicall Satyre and Shakespeare's Troilus and Cressida.* San Marino, 1938.

LAWRENCE, W. W. 'Troilus, Cressida, and Thersites.' *MLR*, XXXVII, 1942, 422–37.

SPENCER, T. *Shakespeare and the Nature of Man*, New York, 1942, pp. 109–121.

REYNOLDS, G. F. '*Troilus and Cressida* on the Elizabethan Stage' in *J. Q. Adams Memorial Studies*, Washington, 1948, pp. 229–38.

KNIGHTS, L. C. '*Troilus and Cressida* Again.' *Scrutiny*, XVIII, 1952.

WHITAKER, V. K. *Shakespeare's Use of Learning*, San Marino, 1953, pp. 194–223.

PRESSON, R. K. *Shakespeare's Troilus and Cressida and the Legends of Troy.* Madison, 1953.

NOWOTTNY, W. M. T. ' "Opinion" and "Value" in *Troilus and Cressida.*' *EC*, IV, 1954, 282–96.

KERMODE, F. 'Opinion, Truth and Value.' *EC*, V, 1955, 181–7.

TRAVERSI, D. A. *An Approach to Shakespeare*, 2nd edn., New York, 1956, pp. 63–81.

BOWDEN, W. R. 'The Human Shakespeare and *Troilus and Cressida.*' *ShQ*, VIII, 1957, 166–77.

BRADBROOK, M. C. 'What Shakespeare Did to Chaucer's *Troilus and Criseyde.*' *ShQ*, IX, 1958, 310–19.

KNIGHTS, L. C. *Some Shakespearean Themes*, 1959, pp. 65–83.

KNOWLAND, A. S. 'Troilus and Cressida.' *ShQ*, X, 1959, 353–65.

ALL'S WELL THAT ENDS WELL

First edition: First printed, 1623, in the FIRST FOLIO.

Modern editions: Arden, ed. Brigstocke (1904, 1929); Yale, ed. A. E. Case (1926); New Cambridge, ed. Quiller-Couch and Dover Wilson (1929); New Arden, ed. Hunter (1960).

CRITICAL STUDIES

DELIUS, N. 'Shakespeare's *All's Well* and Paynter's *Giletta of Narbonne.*' *ShJ*, XXII, 1887.

KRAPP, G. P. 'Parolles' in *Shakespearian Studies*, ed. Matthews and Thorndike. New York, 1916, pp. 291–300.

LEGOUIS, E. 'La comtesse de Roussillon.' *English*, I, 1937, 399–404.

BRADBROOK, M. C. 'Virtue is the True Nobility: a Study of the Structure of *All's Well.*' *RES*, New Ser., I, 1950, 298–301.

WILSON, H. S. 'Dramatic Emphasis in *All's Well.*' *HLQ*, XIII, 1949–50, 217–40.

LEECH, C. 'The Theme of Ambition in *All's Well.*' *ELH*, XXI, 1954, 17–29.

CARTER, A. H. 'In Defense of Bertram.' *ShQ*, VII, 1956, 21–31.

KNIGHT, G. W. 'The Third Eye: an essay on *All's Well*,' in *The Sovereign Flower.* 1958

SCHOFF, F. G. 'Claudio, Bertram, and a Note on Interpretation.' *ShQ*, X, 1959, 11–23.

MEASURE FOR MEASURE

First edition: First printed, 1623, in the FIRST FOLIO.

Modern editions: Arden, ed. Hart (1905); New Cambridge, ed. Quiller-Couch and Dover Wilson (1922); Yale, ed. Durham (1922).

CRITICAL STUDIES

PATER, W. '*Measure for Measure*' in *Appreciations*, 1889.

SYMONS, A. '*Measure for Measure*' in *Studies in Elizabethan Drama*. 1920.

KOSZUL, A. 'La Technique de Shakespeare étudiée dans le premier Acte de *Measure for Measure*.' *Revue de l'Enseignement des Langues vivantes*, XLIV, 1927.

DURHAM, W. H. '*Measure for Measure* as a Measure for Critics' in *California Essays in Criticism*, Berkeley, 1929.

KNIGHT, G. W. '*Measure for Measure* and the Gospels' in *The Wheel of Fire*. 1930, 1947.

CHAMBERS, R. W. '*Measure for Measure*' in *Man's Unconquerable Mind*. 1939.

BRADBROOK, M. C. 'Authority, Truth, and Justice in *Measure for Measure*.' *RES*, XVII, 1941, 385–99.

KNIGHTS, L. C. 'The Ambiguity of *Measure for Measure*.' *Scrutiny*, X, 1942.

BATTENHOUSE, R. W. '*Measure for Measure* and Christian Doctrine of the Atonement.' *PMLA*, LXI, 1946, 1029–59.

DODDS, W. M. T. 'The Character of Angelo in *Measure for Measure*.' *MLR*, XLI, 1946, 246–55.

MAXWELL, J. C. '*Measure for Measure*: a Footnote to Recent Criticism.' *The Downside Review*, January, 1947.

McGINN, D. J. 'The Precise Angelo', in *J. Q. Adams Memorial Studies*, Washington, 1948 pp. 129–39.

MAXWELL, J. C. 'Creon and Angelo: a Parallel Study.' *Greece and Rome*, XVIII, 1949, 32–36.

POPE, E. M. 'The Renaissance Background of *Measure for Measure*.' *ShS*, II, 1949, 66–82.

LEECH, C. 'The "Meaning" of *Measure for Measure*.' *ShS*, III, 1950, 66–73.

HARDING, D. P. 'Elizabethan Betrothals and *Measure for Measure*.' *JEGP*, XLIX, 1950, 139–58.

SMITH, R. M. 'Interpretations of *Measure for Measure*.' *ShQ*, I, 1950.

LEAVIS, F. R. '*Measure for Measure*' in *The Common Pursuit*. 1952.

LASCELLES, M. *Shakespeare's Measure for Measure*. 1953.

TRAVERSI, D. A. '*Measure for Measure*' in *An Approach to Shakespeare*, 2nd edn., New York, 1956, pp. 107–25.

LAWRENCE, W. W. '*Measure for Measure* and Lucio.' *ShQ*, IX, 1958, 443–53.

LEVER, J. W. 'The Date of *Measure for Measure*.' *ShQ*, X, 1959, 381–8.

MERCHANT, W. M. 'Measure for Measure: an Essay in Visual Interpretation.' in Shakespeare and the Artist, 1959, pp. 221–32.

SCHANZER, E. 'The Marriage-Contracts in Measure for Measure.' ShS, XIII, 1960, 81–9.

TIMON OF ATHENS

First edition: First printed, 1623, in the FIRST FOLIO.

Modern editions: Arden, ed. Deighton (1905, 1929); Yale, ed. Williams (1919); New Temple, ed. Ridley (1934); New Cambridge, ed. Maxwell (1957); New Arden, ed. Oliver (1959).

CRITICAL STUDIES

BRADLEY, A. C. 'King Lear and Timon of Athens' in Shakespearian Tragedy. 1904.

CLEMONS, W. H. 'The Sources of Timon of Athens.' Princeton University Bulletin, 1903–4, 208–23.

ADAMS, J. Q. 'The Timon Plays.' JEGP, IX, 1910, 506–24.

PARROTT, T. M. The Problem of Timon of Athens. Shakespeare Association Pamphlet, 1923.

KNIGHT, G. W. 'The Pilgrimage of Hate: an Essay on Timon of Athens', in The Wheel of Fire. 1930, 1947.

BOND, R. W. 'Lucian and Boiardo in Timon of Athens.' MLR, XXVI, 1931, 52–68.

DRAPER, J. W. 'The Theme of Timon of Athens.' MLR, XXIX, 1934, 20–31.

PHILLIPS, J. E. The State in Shakespeare's Greek and Roman Plays. New York, 1940, pp. 112–46.

ELLIS-FERMOR, U. 'Timon of Athens: an Unfinished Play.' RES, XVIII, 1942, 270–83; and in Shakespeare the Dramatist, 1961, pp. 158–76.

CAMPBELL, O. J. Shakespeare's Satire. New York, 1943, pp. 168–97.

COLLINS, A. S. 'Timon of Athens: a Reconsideration.' RES, XXII, 1946, 96–108.

PETTET, E. C. 'Timon of Athens: the Disruption of Feudal Morality.' RES, XXIII, 1947, 321–36.

MAXWELL, J. C. 'Timon of Athens.' Scrutiny, XV, 1948, 195–208.

FARNHAM, W. Shakespeare's Tragic Frontier. Berkeley and Los Angeles, 1950, pp. 39–77.

LEECH, C. 'Timon and After' in Shakespeare's Tragedies, 1950, pp. 113–36.

SPENCER, T. J. B. 'Shakespeare Learns the Value of Money: Shakespeare at Work on Timon of Athens.' ShS, VI, 1953, 75–8.

BONNARD, G. A. 'Note sur les sources de *Timon of Athens.*' *Études Anglaises*, VII, 1954.

GOLDSMITH, R. H. 'Did Shakespeare use the old Timon Comedy?' *ShQ*, IX, 1958, 31–8.

MERCHANT, W. M. '*Timon of Athens* and the Visual Conceit' in *Shakespeare and the Artist*, 1959, pp. 167–77.

HONIGMANN, E. A. J. '*Timon of Athens.*' *ShQ*, XII, 1961, 3–20.

31/25